Wok &
Stir-fry

Everyday recipes to enjoy

beef stir-fry

ingredients

SERVES 4

2 tbsp vegetable or groundnut
    oil
2 medium red onions, sliced
    thinly
2 garlic cloves, chopped
2.5-cm/1-inch piece ginger,
    cut into thin sticks
2 x 115-g/4-oz beef fillets,
    sliced thinly
1 green pepper, deseeded
    and sliced
150 g/5^1/$_2$ oz canned
    bamboo shoots
115 g/4 oz beansprouts
2 tbsp Thai magic paste
    (see below)
1 tbsp Thai red curry paste
handful of fresh coriander,
    chopped
a few sprigs fresh Thai basil
boiled rice, to serve

thai magic paste

whole bulb of garlic, peeled
bunch of fresh coriander
    leaves and roots,
    roughly chopped
55 g/2 oz white peppercorns

method

1 To make the Thai magic paste, pulse all the ingredients briefly in a blender or food processor to form a thick paste, or pound with a pestle until well mixed. Store in the refrigerator for 3–4 days or freeze in small amounts.

2 Heat the oil in a wok and stir-fry the onions, garlic and ginger for 1 minute.

3 Add the beef strips and stir-fry over high heat until browned all over.

4 Add the vegetables, magic paste and curry paste and cook for 2–3 minutes until blended and cooked.

5 Stir in the coriander and basil and serve immediately with rice.

beef chop suey

ingredients

SERVES 4

450 g/1 lb ribeye or sirloin
   steak, finely sliced
1 head of broccoli, cut into
   small florets
2 tbsp vegetable or groundnut
   oil
1 onion, finely sliced
2 celery stalks, finely sliced
   diagonally
225 g/8 oz mangetout, sliced
   in half lengthways
55 g/2 oz fresh or canned
   bamboo shoots, rinsed
   and julienned (if using
   fresh shoots, boil in water
   first for 30 minutes)
8 water chestnuts, finely
   sliced
225 g/8 oz finely sliced
   mushrooms
1 tbsp oyster sauce
1 tsp salt
freshly cooked rice, to serve

marinade

1 tbsp Shaoxing rice wine
pinch of white pepper
pinch of salt
1 tbsp light soy sauce
1/2 tsp sesame oil

method

1 Combine all the marinade ingredients in a bowl and marinate the beef for at least 20 minutes. Blanch the broccoli in a large pan of boiling water for 30 seconds. Drain and set aside.

2 In a preheated wok, heat 1 tablespoon of the oil and stir-fry the beef until the colour has changed. Remove and set aside.

3 In the clean wok, heat the remaining oil and stir-fry the onion for 1 minute. Add the celery and broccoli and cook for 2 minutes. Add the mangetout, bamboo shoots, water chestnuts and mushrooms and cook for 1 minute. Add the beef, then season with the oyster sauce and salt and serve with freshly cooked rice.

pork lo mein

ingredients

SERVES 4–6

175 g/6 oz boneless lean
   pork, shredded
225 g/8 oz egg noodles
1¹/₂ tbsp vegetable or
   groundnut oil
2 tsp finely chopped garlic
1 tsp finely chopped fresh
   ginger
1 carrot, julienned
225 g/8 oz finely
   sliced mushrooms
1 green pepper, thinly sliced
1 tsp salt
175 ml/6 fl oz hot chicken
   stock
200 g/7 oz beansprouts,
   trimmed
2 tbsp finely chopped spring
   onion

marinade

1 tsp light soy sauce
dash of sesame oil
pinch of white pepper

method

1 Combine all the marinade ingredients in a bowl and marinate the pork for at least 20 minutes.

2 Cook the noodles according to the directions on the packet. When cooked, drain and then set aside.

3 In a preheated wok, heat 1 teaspoon of the oil and stir-fry the pork until the colour has changed. Remove and set aside.

4 In the clean wok, heat the remaining oil and stir-fry the garlic and ginger until fragrant. Add the carrot and cook for 1 minute, then add the mushrooms and cook for 1 minute. Toss in the pepper and cook for 1 minute. Add the pork, salt and stock and heat through. Finally, toss in the noodles, followed by the beansprouts, and stir well. Sprinkle with the spring onion and serve.

wok-fried jumbo prawns in spicy sauce

ingredients

SERVES 4

3 tbsp vegetable or groundnut oil

450 g/1 lb raw king prawns, deveined but unpeeled

2 tsp finely chopped fresh ginger

1 tsp finely chopped garlic

1 tbsp chopped spring onion

2 tbsp chilli bean sauce

1 tsp Shaoxing rice wine

1 tsp sugar

1/2 tsp light soy sauce

1–2 tbsp chicken stock

method

1 In a preheated wok, heat the oil, then toss in the prawns and stir-fry over high heat for about 4 minutes. Arrange the prawns on the sides of the wok out of the oil, then throw in the ginger and garlic and stir until fragrant. Add the spring onion and chilli bean sauce. Stir the prawns into this mixture.

2 Lower the heat slightly and add the rice wine, sugar, soy sauce and a little chicken stock. Cover and cook for a further minute. Serve immediately.

spicy scallops with lime & chilli

ingredients

SERVES 4

16 large scallops, shelled

1 tbsp butter

1 tbsp vegetable oil

1 tsp crushed garlic

1 tsp grated fresh ginger

1 bunch of spring onions,
    finely sliced

finely grated rind of 1 lime

1 small fresh red chilli,
    deseeded and very finely
    chopped

3 tbsp lime juice

lime wedges, to garnish

freshly cooked rice, to serve

method

1 Using a sharp knife, trim the scallops to remove any black intestine, then wash and pat dry with kitchen paper. Separate the corals from the white parts, then slice each white part in half horizontally, making 2 circles.

2 Heat the butter and oil in a preheated wok. Add the garlic and ginger and stir-fry for 1 minute without browning. Add the spring onions and stir-fry for 1 minute.

3 Add the scallops and continue stir-frying over high heat for 4–5 minutes. Stir in the lime rind, chilli and lime juice and cook for a further 1 minute.

4 Transfer the scallops to serving plates, then spoon over the cooking juices and garnish with lime wedges. Serve hot with freshly cooked rice.

stir-fried squid with hot black bean sauce

ingredients

SERVES 4

750 g/1 lb 10 oz squid, cleaned and tentacles discarded

1 large red pepper, deseeded

115 g/4 oz mangetout

1 head of pak choi

3 tbsp black bean sauce

1 tbsp Thai fish sauce

1 tbsp rice wine or dry sherry

1 tbsp dark soy sauce

1 tsp brown sugar

1 tsp cornflour

1 tbsp water

1 tbsp corn oil

1 tsp sesame oil

1 small fresh red Thai chilli, chopped

1 garlic clove, finely chopped

1 tsp grated fresh ginger

2 spring onions, chopped

method

1 Cut the squid body cavities into quarters lengthways. Use the tip of a small, sharp knife to score a diamond pattern into the flesh, without cutting all the way through. Pat dry with kitchen paper.

2 Cut the pepper into long, thin slices. Cut the mangetout in half diagonally. Coarsely shred the pak choi.

3 Mix the black bean sauce, fish sauce, rice wine, soy sauce and sugar together in a bowl. Blend the cornflour with the water and stir into the other sauce ingredients. Reserve the mixture until required.

4 Heat the oils in a preheated wok. Add the chilli, garlic, ginger and spring onions and stir-fry for 1 minute. Add the pepper slices and stir-fry for 2 minutes.

5 Add the squid and stir-fry over high heat for a further 1 minute. Stir in the mangetout and pak choi and stir for a further 1 minute, or until wilted.

6 Stir in the sauce mixture and cook, stirring constantly, for 2 minutes, or until the sauce thickens and clears. Serve immediately.

sweet-&-sour vegetables with cashew nuts

ingredients

SERVES 4

1 tbsp vegetable or groundnut oil

1 tsp chilli oil

2 onions, sliced

2 carrots, sliced thinly

2 courgettes, sliced thinly

115 g/4 oz head of broccoli, cut into florets

115 g/4 oz white mushrooms, sliced

115 g/4 oz small pak choi, halved

2 tbsp jaggery or soft light brown sugar

2 tbsp Thai soy sauce

1 tbsp rice vinegar

55 g/2 oz cashew nuts

method

1 Heat the vegetable oil and the chilli oil in a wok and stir-fry the onions for 1–2 minutes, until they start to soften.

2 Add the carrots, courgettes and broccoli, and stir-fry for 2–3 minutes. Add the mushrooms, pak choi, sugar, soy sauce and rice vinegar and stir-fry for 1–2 minutes.

3 Meanwhile, dry-fry or toast the cashew nuts. Sprinkle the cashews over the stir-fry and serve immediately.

mixed vegetables with quick-fried basil

ingredients

SERVES 4

2 tbsp vegetable or groundnut
   oil
2 garlic cloves, chopped
1 onion, sliced
115 g/4 oz baby corn cobs,
   cut in half diagonally
1/2 cucumber, peeled, halved,
   deseeded and sliced
225 g/8 oz canned water
   chestnuts, drained
   and rinsed
55 g/2 oz mangetout,
   trimmed
115 g/4 oz shiitake
   mushrooms, halved
1 red pepper, deseeded and
   sliced thinly
1 tbsp jaggery or soft light
   brown sugar
2 tbsp Thai soy sauce
1 tbsp fish sauce
1 tbsp rice vinegar
boiled rice, to serve

quick-fried basil

vegetable or groundnut oil,
   for cooking
8–12 sprigs fresh Thai basil

method

1 Heat the oil in a wok and stir-fry the garlic and onion for 1–2 minutes. Add the corn cobs, cucumber, water chestnuts, mangetout, mushrooms and red pepper and stir-fry for 2–3 minutes, until starting to soften.

2 Add the sugar, soy sauce, fish sauce and vinegar and gradually bring to the boil. Simmer for 1–2 minutes.

3 Meanwhile, heat the oil for the basil in a wok and, when hot, add the basil sprigs. Cook for 20–30 seconds, until crisp. Remove with a slotted spoon and drain on kitchen paper.

4 Garnish the vegetable stir-fry with the crispy basil and serve immediately, with the boiled rice.

egg-fried rice with vegetables & crispy onions

ingredients

SERVES 4

4 tbsp vegetable or groundnut
   oil
2 garlic cloves, chopped
   finely
2 fresh red chillies, deseeded
   and chopped
115 g/4 oz mushrooms,
   sliced
55 g/2 oz mangetout, halved
55 g/2 oz baby corn cobs,
   halved
3 tbsp Thai soy sauce
1 tbsp jaggery or soft light
   brown sugar
a few fresh Thai basil leaves,
   plus extra sprigs to garnish
350 g/12 oz rice, cooked and
   cooled
2 eggs, beaten
2 onions, sliced

method

1 Heat half the oil in a wok and sauté the garlic and chillies for 2–3 minutes.

2 Add the mushrooms, mangetout and corn and stir-fry for 2–3 minutes before adding the soy sauce, sugar and basil. Stir in the rice.

3 Push the mixture to one side of the wok and add the eggs to the bottom. Stir until lightly set before combining into the rice mixture.

4 Heat the remaining oil in another wok and sauté the onions until crispy and brown. Serve the rice topped with the onions and garnished with basil sprigs.